The Life Story of James Dewitt Yancey

Written by Maureen Yancey-Smith, Diana V. Boardley-Wise, MBA
and CQ Wilder M.ED
Illustrated by Tokio Aoyama
Cover Art by Shawn Wise & Louis Claveria

Thank You For Your Support!

JDILLAMERCH.COM

ISBN 978-1-61225-349-7

©Copyright 2016 Maureen Yancey-Smith,
Diana V.Boardley-Wise, MBA and CQ Wilder M.ED
All rights reserved

No part of this publication may be reproduced in any form or stored, transmitted or recorded by any means without the written permission of the author.

Published by Mirror Publishing
Fort Payne, AL 35967

Printed in the USA.

J Dilla is one of the best producers to ever do it and his beats will carry on forever! He was a hard worker who stayed true to his craft which influences and inspires me daily. I learned from my father how hard work can take you far and this gives me confidence that as long as I put my mind to it, I can achieve greatness. J Dilla will always be a part of me. He was my father and will live in me forever.

-- Ja'Mya Sherran Yancey

J Dilla will be king of the beats forever! I am very proud to be his daughter because he was a good person and his music has inspired the lives of many people. Someday, I would love to follow in his footsteps by impacting people's lives either in the music industry or the field of criminal justice. -- Ty'Monae Whitlow

James' accomplishments have inspired me to set and reach all my goals. He made it one of his missions to show the youth the power of never giving up no matter your current situation. No matter your background or obstacles, you can always succeed. James was a hardworking man who worked everyday to get to where he needed to be and is now being recognized all over the world for it. Not only is he one of the best producers but also, a positive role model and I'm proud to call him my uncle.

-- Faith Lamb

I dedicate this book to the art of parenting and the gift of love that bonds a parent to their child forever. I also dedicate this book to education, the arts, and music. Music, a form of language that is universal, is a gift that everyone can share. Music was not only James Dewitt Yancey's love, but his gift to the world. -- Maureen Yancey-Smith

This book is dedicated to all the children around the world. Love is music and music is love. One love to all my family and friends. To my grandma and Suggie, you will always have a special place in my heart until we meet again.

-- Diana Boardley-Wise, MBA

I thank my mom, P. Robinson, for her love and dedication, Jon B. for making great music, and Tif and Teeny for being amazing best friends. -- CQ Wilder, M.ED

James Dewitt Yancey was born on February 7, 1974 in Detroit, Michigan to Maureen Yancey, a former opera singer and known as Ma Dukes, and Dewitt Yancey, a jazz bassist. Ma Dukes would read books and sing to her unborn baby while his father played the upright bass. Neither realized these first introductions to literature and music would later create one of the most influential producers in Hip Hop, R&B, Jazz, and Neo Soul.

Infant James wasn't much of a sleeper. With so many beats and music floating in his young, developing brain, how could he? The exhausted Yancey parents tried numerous ways to get him to sleep, but to no avail. Only when his father played the upright bass, he fell asleep instantly, astonishing both.

At three months old, James' father continued playing the physically demanding upright bass to his son. While switching effortlessly among the strings and creating new bars, James would match the sounds from the upright bass to his own voice, creating a perfect pitch.

James always enjoyed looking at books and would hold them open, attempting to read the words. Ma Dukes always read books to him, recognizing the importance of introducing education and its positive impact at a young age.

James would always observe and listen to his father while he taught others music lessons. In a sound-proofed room, he was introduced to instruments including the piano, keyboard, court organ, and the Reel to Reel tape recorder to name a few. He would always showcase his perfect pitch to others during these sessions.

James loved listening to James Brown records in his playpen. Before he could even walk, he would pull his little body up using the nets of the pen and dance the night away. While his mother stood nervously watching, others would be in awe that not only was he a quiet baby, but a great dancer. He always instinctively knew that his favorite songs were about to play.

Around the age of two, James was a collector of music. He would shop at a local record store where they would always play music catered to his musical likeness. He was never afraid to voice his opinion about music he disliked; it had to really move and touch him for him to love and listen to it.

He would gather the 45 records he wanted to purchase and carry them on his arm and wrists, proud of his growing collection. James knew the music store was a special place so he would always wear a hat, sunglasses, and a jacket. The sunglasses always matched the hat, which always matched the jacket. He had so much style.

Harmony Park was another favorite place for James growing up. While Ma Dukes worked in their family-owned restaurant, father and son would go to the park every day after work. James loved the array of people who visited the park and enjoyed walking around the roundabout, sitting on the benches, and mostly, playing his music.

A large audience would crowd around young James while he spun music in Harmony Park. Observing the smiles from his fans, he studied the reactions on their faces and how they responded to the music he spun with praise and compliments. Even though he was unable to read, he received numerous musical requests and because he knew his content, he always pleased the onlookers and listeners with older music of their taste.

Before he was five years old, James began taking piano lessons at a music school. He was obedient and listened during practices. He didn't enjoy the school, but he endured it. He later began taking classes with the professor of music from his church at a new school on Saturdays where he excelled and mastered the piano.

Kindergarten was very interesting for James. He learned many new things and met new friends. Later that year he graduated looking like a grown little man in his white cap and gown.

At the age of eight, James was an official cub scout. He liked his uniform and participating in cadences. Music was everything to him so he gravitated to the patterns and songs the cubs practiced. His mother always tried her best to expose him to other things to motivate and improve his talents. She was raising a well-rounded son.

Around nine years old, he began learning the drums at school. That Christmas, he wanted a set for himself to practice at home. Ma Dukes knew that a kid drum set would not be sufficient for the talented James, so they invested in the best snare drum set they could find. He worked those drums like he was playing in a professional band.

He was a talented, school contest-award winning writer at the same age. He practiced his writing skills at home, where his family held sibling contests. He was charged to memorize his writing by heart along with the appropriate expressions and act out the story in front of the family. He enjoyed telling his stories and reliving them for others.

Mrs. McConnell was a beloved music teacher of James'. She showed pictures of instruments and he picked what he wanted to learn: the cello. Even though he was small in stature, he had a strong heart to play. He also learned how to play the baritone and played them simultaneously. He was developing into a master of the arts.

He played in the school band and orchestra and would run from one performance to another in the same night at concerts and music festivals. Mrs. McConnell only allowed him to do so as long as he was able to stay organized and attentive. He never had a problem with that; he had such a high aptitude and outstanding musical skills.

When he was thirteen years old, he observed his sister learning the flute. Because he had such an ear and talent for music, he took that same flute and manual to his room and fifteen minutes later, came back downstairs playing it fluently without stumbling. "The notes are the same as the drum notes," he explained nonchalantly to a shocked Ma Dukes.

James became a Junior Cadet Police Officer at the age of fourteen and hated every minute of it. He did enjoy welding, working on anything electrical, and fixing planes. Ma Dukes would pick him up after school because he wouldn't be caught dead in public wearing his uniform.

Ma Dukes knew his hatred toward his uniform and dislike of the school he attended where he was an A student. She bribed him by buying different colored silk shirts and had them waiting for him weekly when she gave him rides home when he wore his uniform. He later took on the name DJ Silk due to his love of silk shirts and music.

Al Green held notes for a very long time with exaggeration while he sang. Illa J, younger brother of James, remembers, "My brother and I would compete against each other to see who could hold Al Green's notes the longest. The song *Love and Happiness* was a true favorite. We would extend the vocal runs to mimic Al Green and do it at the same time to see who could hold their breathe long enough."

On the weekends, DJ Silk (aka James) would be found spinning records. While the Yancey parents waited outside in their car for his performance to end, DJ Silk spun records inside for parties, weddings, and anything and everything that needed a DJ and music.

25

Not everything was business related for James though. He was still a young teenager looking for fun. He, along with Frank-N-Dank, and other friends would pack the Yancey car to be escorted to Northland Roller Rink. They loved skating and listening to the music at the rink.

James would change his name from DJ Silk (aka Jay Dee) to J Dilla. He was later introduced to a local, talented musician named Amp Fiddler. He taught J Dilla how to use the MPC 60, Reel to Reel, and other instruments at his home. The two collaborated on a song with many others titled *Ghost Town Till the Break of Day* and Amp Fiddler also helped T3, Baatin, and J Dilla, the founding members of Slum Village, in his home studio.

At the time unbeknownst to J Dilla and Slum Village, Amp Fiddler's guidance and support would later help launch musical careers taking a local group into mainstream status. Also, J Dilla would later evolve into a multi-genre, hit making producer in high demand.

To be continued

CPSIA information can be obtained
at www.ICGtesting.com
Printed in the USA
BVHW02n2349260818
525562BV00002B/6/P